Learning
to Get
Along®

Be Honest and Tell the Truth

Cheri J. Meiners, M.Ed.
Illustrated by Meredith Johnson

free spirit
PUBLISHING®

Library of Congress Cataloging-in-Publication Data
Meiners, Cheri J., 1957–
    Be honest and tell the truth / Cheri J. Meiners ; illustrated by Meredith Johnson.
        p. cm. — (Learning to get along)
    ISBN-13: 978-1-57542-258-9
    ISBN-10: 1-57542-258-1
    1. Honesty—Juvenile literature. I. Johnson, Meredith. II. Title.
BJ1533.H7M45 2007
179'.9—dc22
                                                                                              2007012934

ISBN: 978-1-57542-258-9

Free Spirit Publishing does not have control over or assume responsibility for author or third-party websites and their content.

Reading Level Grade 1; Interest Level Ages 4–8;
Fountas & Pinnell Guided Reading Level H

Cover and interior design by Marieka Heinlen
Edited by Marjorie Lisovskis

20 19 18 17 16 15 14
Printed in China
R18860219

Free Spirit Publishing Inc.
6325 Sandburg Road, Suite 100
Minneapolis, MN 55427-3674
(612) 338-2068
help4kids@freespirit.com
www.freespirit.com

Dedication

To Andrea, Julia, Daniel,
James, Erika, Kara, Luke,
and especially David,
for your lives
of integrity

Acknowledgments

I wish to thank Meredith Johnson, whose charming illustrations resonate so well with the text, and Marieka Heinlen for the exuberant design. I appreciate Judy Galbraith and the entire Free Spirit family for their dedicated support of the series. I am especially grateful to Margie Lisovskis for her diplomatic style as well as her talented editing. I also recognize Mary Jane Weiss, Ph.D., for her expertise and gift in teaching social skills. Lastly, I thank my fantastic family—who are all an inspiration to me.

I'm learning to tell the difference
between what is true
and what isn't.

I may have an idea
that something is true

or that it's the right thing to do.

When I'm honest,
I act the way I feel is right and true.

I can feel good about my choices.

I'm treating someone the way
I want to be treated.

I can be honest with my words.

I can decide to always tell the truth.

I can look a person in the eye
and politely say what I know.

I can find something nice to say.

I can decide how much to say
and when to say it.

I can think about how the other person might feel.

Some things are private
or meant to be a surprise.

I show respect for a person
when I keep these things to myself.

I can talk to a grown-up I trust whenever I need help

or I'm not sure what to do.

If I joke or pretend with someone,

I can let the person know I'm just playing.

And I can stop joking if it isn't fun for everyone.

I can have courage and tell the truth when I make a mistake.

I won't blame someone else.

I might find a way to fix my mistake

and make things better.

I can do my own work.

I can be honest
even when no one else knows or sees.

I can keep my promises.

When I do what I say I will,
I can make my words come true.

People can depend on me.

I can show respect for people
and their things.

I won't touch something that isn't mine unless I get permission.

If I find something that doesn't belong to me, I can try to return it.

Being honest is worth more to me than having something that's not really mine.

I want to treat people fairly

so that they can believe me
and trust me.

When I'm honest and tell the truth,
I feel good about myself.

I'm trying to be the best
that I can be.

Ways to Reinforce the Ideas in
Be Honest and Tell the Truth

Be Honest and Tell the Truth teaches children about telling the truth and acting honestly even when tempted to be deceptive in order to avoid consequences. Honesty requires respect for oneself and others, personal responsibility, and fairness to others. As they practice living honestly, children may develop character traits of courage, dependability, and unselfishness. Here are terms you may want to discuss:

courage: bravery; when you show courage, you do something you believe is right, even if it is hard or you feel afraid

depend: to trust or count on; if people can depend on you, they trust that you'll do what you say

honest: truthful and fair

promise: to say that you will do something and really mean it; when you keep a promise, you do what you said you would do

respect: true politeness toward others; when you show respect to people, you show that you think they are important

As you read each page spread, ask children:

- What's happening in this picture?

Here are additional questions you might discuss:

Pages 1–5

- *(point to page 1)* Do you think the story the teacher is reading is about something that's *real* or *not real?* Could it really happen? How do you know?

- Think of a time you told someone the truth or did the right thing. What happened? How did you feel?

- How do you feel when people are honest with you? How do you think other people feel when you are honest?

Pages 6–15

- Why is it important to tell the truth? What can happen when people lie? *(They may start telling more and more lies; other people might stop believing or trusting them.)*

- Can you think of a time when it would be better *not* to say everything you think or know? *(when it might embarrass the other person; when it is something private that someone else doesn't want to share)*

- Do you think you should keep a secret that someone tells you? Why or why not? *(You may want to address when it is and is not safe to keep a secret.)*

- When is a time that you should tell an adult you trust about a problem even if the person says not to tell? *(If you feel uncomfortable, if something isn't safe, if you think someone may get hurt; it may be helpful to discuss the difference between tattling to get someone in trouble or to get attention and telling an adult so no one is hurt and everyone stays safe.)*

Pages 16–25

- How is it honest to do your own work?

- Think of a time you did something you said you would. How did you feel? How did the other person feel?

- Why is it important to be honest even when no one else knows? What person always knows when you are honest?

- Have you ever made a mistake and told the truth about it? How did that feel?

- What is a way that you can respect other people's things?

Pages 26–31

- *(Point to page 26.)* What do you think the girl plans to do with the money? What would *you* do?

- Think of a person you know who is honest. How do you feel around that person? How would you like people to feel when they are around *you?*

Fostering Honest Behavior

Your response to children's behavior can influence and shape it. Here are some tips that may be helpful:

- **Teach the expected behavior.** It is typical for young children to confuse reality and fantasy; their exaggerations may reflect their true perception of a situation. Gaining a sense of what is true or morally right takes time and experience. Teach appropriate behavior on a regular basis, and ask questions to see if the child understands the expected behavior.

- **Set consequences.** At a quiet time, discuss the consequences that will happen as a result of lying or cheating, such as the temporary loss of a privilege.

- **Speak calmly.** When there are breaches of honesty, talk about the problem calmly. Let the child know that you are aware of the true situation. Don't question, accuse, or moralize at that moment about the importance of honesty. These responses lead to defensiveness, strain the relationship, and make it more difficult for the child to be honest with you. Be matter-of-fact in following through with consequences.

- **Give meaningful praise.** Model appropriate behavior, and notice and acknowledge the examples of honesty that you observe in the child. If a child admits a mistake, praise the child for telling the truth about what happened. You can also praise other children who behave appropriately so that the child can observe and anticipate this kind of positive reinforcement. Positive attention helps children learn to trust you and the safe environment you create and allows room for children to grow and become trustworthy.

Honesty Games

Read this book often with your child or group of children. Once children are familiar with the book, refer to it when teachable moments arise involving both positive behavior and problems related to being honest. Notice and comment when children show that they understand what is true or honest and when they speak or act honestly. In addition, use the following activities to reinforce children's understanding of why and how to be honest.

Honesty Partner Role Plays

Preparation: Write a number 1 on two different index cards. Continue numbering in this way (1, 1; 2, 2; 3, 3; and so forth) until you have as many cards as there are children in your group. Put the cards in a bag. On other index cards, write individual scenarios similar to the following. Place the cards in a separate bag.

Sample Scenarios:

- Han wants to play with his brother Li's favorite toy. Li isn't home.
- Tessa ate a cookie after her mom said not to. Mom asks Tessa if she ate a cookie.
- Trish doesn't know an answer on a test. She thinks maybe the person next to her knows it.
- Cody tells his friend Gus a secret and asks Gus not to tell anyone.
- Cami didn't do her homework. Her teacher asks where it is.

Have children form pairs by drawing a number card and finding the person with the same number. Help each pair of children draw a scenario card and read it aloud. Ask, "What would be an honest thing to do?" Have children work together to decide on an honest ending. Have or help the children role-play the scenario.

"Hooked" on Honesty

Materials: Colored construction paper, scissors, pen or marker, paper clips, stick 3'–5' long, string, strong magnet

Cut out several fish shapes from construction paper. Write a scenario on each fish and attach a paper clip. (Use the scenarios above or make up your own.) Tie the string to the stick; attach a magnet to the string end. Have children "fish" for a scenario and then respond to the question, "What would be an honest thing to do?"

"Treasure" Honesty

Preparation: Have one child (or a small group of children) leave the room while other children remain with you. Hide a box containing a small item or treat for each child, such as a sticker, pencil, or balloon.

Directions: Bring everyone back together and have the returning child or children ask the children who remained in the room questions about where the "treasure" is hidden. (Examples: "Is it underneath something?" "What color is the thing it's underneath?") Tell the children to respond honestly. When the treasure is found, everyone gets to share it. Discuss the fact that we trust others when they are honest and that being trustworthy benefits everyone. Rotate the child or group who looks for the treasure when you play again.

Variations: Instead of placing treats or objects in the box, write a brief note for each child about something honest or admirable you've noticed. Fold and label each note with the child's name. Or write a single group privilege on an index card and place it inside the box; this might be an activity such as extra time at a favorite learning center, a nature walk, or an art project.

Telling the Truth—Who "Nose"?

Materials: Craft knife, white paper plate for each child, colored construction paper cut in 8" x 3" strips, tape, glue sticks, scissors, index cards, pen, crayons or markers, yarn, whiteboard and magnets; *optional:* copy of a simple telling of the story "Pinocchio"

Preparation: Using a craft knife, put a 2"–3" vertical slit in the center of each plate. Prepare noses by folding the construction paper strips in half lengthwise, taping or gluing them shut, and rounding off one end with scissors for the tip of the nose. Make word cards labeled "True" and "False." Make several true-false scenario cards by writing true or false statements on index cards. (Examples: "It is snowing outside." "Cows have four legs." "Steven is wearing green.")

Directions: Before beginning the activity, read or talk about the story of Pinocchio, whose nose grew every time he told a lie. Then have or help each child make a Pinocchio face by coloring in eyes and a mouth and gluing on yarn for hair. Show children how to put the nose through the slit. On the back of the plate, help them tape the end piece about 1" from the opening in the plate. When the faces are complete, recall how lying got Pinocchio into trouble. Then have a child draw a true-false scenario card and read the statement. Ask children to move Pinocchio's nose *in* if the statement is true, and *out* if it is false. Put the words "True" and "False" on the whiteboard and allow a child to place the card under the correct heading after it is read. Continue with other scenarios.

Honesty Skits

Preparation: Ask volunteers to tell you a story about a time someone was honest. These can be based in experience or imagination, and can be just a few sentences long. Write down the story in the child's wording. (If you wish, use a tape recorder for the child to dictate the story.) You may want to have on hand a few costumes or props.

Directions: Have children sit with you in a circle on the floor. Explain that they will all have a chance to be actors in skits about honesty. Make sure they understand they will be playing a pretend role. Choose the first story to be enacted and read or have the author read it to the group. (You might also choose to play the recording of the child telling the story.) To choose actors, go around the circle in order. Have the selected children act out the story as you slowly read it again. If the actors wish, they might add in their own dialogue as the story is read. Continue for several stories. Have children return to the same spots in the circle each time until they have all played a part. If you wish, save the written stories in a class or family book where they can be reread and acted out again later with different actors.

Download two supplemental activities at www.freespirit.com/honest; **use the password** 4truth.

Free Spirit's Learning to Get Along® Series

Help children learn, understand, and practice basic social and emotional skills. Real-life situations, diversity, and concrete examples make these read-aloud books appropriate for childcare settings, schools, and the home. *Each book: 40 pp., color illust., PB, 9" x 9", ages 4–8.*

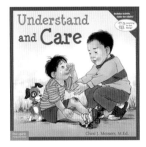

See more
Learning to Get Along®
bilingual editions at
freespirit.com

Each book: 48 pp., color illust., PB, 9" x 9", ages 4–8.